The True Beauty in Me
"Loving Yourself Even When Others Don't"

Shawnda LM Jackson

Printed in the United States of America

ExAlt Prophetic Ministries Publishing

Websites:
http:/wezmichael.wix.com/louisemichael

https://www.facebook.com/authorlouise

"Behold, you are beautiful, my love; behold, you are beautiful; your eyes are doves."

(Song of Solomon 1:15 ESV)

"Whoever gets sense loves his soul; he, who keeps understanding, will discover good."

(Proverbs 19:8 ESV)

Dedication to Zaneta Adams

Zaneta With love this book was inspired by you. Thank you for giving me insight about how Veteran woman and women of Wounded Warriors feel; and deal with certain things. Love can slip away from us so easily and if we do not remember to love ourselves first, we slip away in the cracks. Many of us get to the point where we don't want to make ourselves look good anymore or make others happy because we are not happy.

Veteran woman; Wounded Warriors, and woman all over the world, I am here to tell you that you are beautiful. Thank you again my lovely sister. Continue your work in the Lord and empowering and uplifting many. There is a great reward waiting for you. I love you.

Love Yourself Even When Other's Don't!

Dedication to Mavis J. Foster-Stephens
Front Cover Winner

Mavis this book is dedicated to you from my heart. You are an extraordinary woman. God has allowed you to go through the fire and come out more beautiful than ever before Shining Bright like a Diamond. You are a blessing to many people especially woman all over the world who has struggled with any type of addiction.

You are living proof that God answers prayers and that He can use anyone for his Glory. I admire you because you are strong and you have faith that God will fix anything. Continue to share your story and so much more to millions all across the world so that they can also be free.

You have loved yourself from the inside out causing others to follow suit. Thank you for being such an inspiration and also being a part of the Self Love/Love Yourself Movement that will rock the nation.

I love you for being you, I love you for loving you, and I love you for being a part of this Love Movement!

Contents

Preface

LOVE YOURSELF FIRST

Life can take a toll on us and take us in many directions. Life can also beat us up at times and we lose focus and forget to take care of ourselves. Do you often neglect yourself because you are too busy? Do you sometimes worry and think about how others perceive you? Do you walk out of the house sometimes and forget about your presentation? I wrote this book to remind you know that you are beautiful. You must love yourself first before you can love others. If others don't care or love you back, you should still love yourself no matter what. The point in writing this book is to help you see your beauty inside out. There is a confident person trapped inside of you waiting to breakout and explore the world.

You are an awesome person with great confidence and I want you to see it and go to the next level after reading this book. I have so much to share with you and this could be a great life changing experience for you if you just allow me to penetrate your heart with empowering words of encouragement, wisdom and principles that will help you love and feel beautiful even when others don't feel the same way.

I will help you to see the beauty in you and encourage others as well. If you have ever been in a place where you felt like giving up and letting someone else take the wheel of your life, this book is for you.

Shawnda LM Jackson

Letter to the Reader

Dear Reader,

This book was written to help you realize your worth and to assure you that you are loved and you are beautiful. Everyone needs to know that they are beautiful and they are loved.
I changed my mindset and my life and I am here to help you do the same.

I want you to know that I am happy that you have decided to take a step to changing your life by loving yourself to the fullest. I know it's not easy but it's a start and you will be happy with the end results. I also want to thank you for taking time out of your busy schedule to read my book (smile). You are greatly appreciated and if I saw you in person I would tell you the same thing.
I want you to always remember that you can do anything you set your mind to. You are Beautiful and I love you. Enjoy... HUGS!

Love Always,

Shawnda LM Jackson

One
Loving Yourself to the Fullest
(Love the Greatest of All)

This is Mavis' Story

Dear God,

Help me to get closer to you. I ask you dear Lord to show me a path in my life that will cause me to feel happy again, allowing me to control my responses to heartache and pain. Help me to see your way and walk in my calling oh Lord. I pray this with all that's inside of me Amen.

The true beauty in me means loving myself when others don't. This is the image in which I have created in order that I may love myself to the fullest. This is very different from the image that I have tried to create in the minds of others. This is an image in which I am loved by others. I am a feminist, and being a feminist means the same to me as being black. This means that I must embrace who I am, love and respect myself as though my very own life and the lives of my children depended on it.

In today's society, we are programmed to condemn self-love. We should be condemning selflessness, selfishness, self-hate, and a mixture of other negative things that bring people down. All these things are contrary to self-love. These things prevent us from loving ourselves and others to the fullest. My primary relationship is with myself and then others are mirrors of it as I learn to love myself. I automatically receive the love and appreciation that I desire from others especially if I am committed to loving myself, and living my truth. I will attract others with equal commitment and with my willingness to be intimate with my own deep feelings; it creates space for intimacy with others.

Many people follow me, look up to me, call me for advice, enjoy my company; and my warm welcome of hugs; this brings everything about face. In this, I see my true value and I understand my self-worth. There was a period in my life when I was stripped of everything. At that point I surrendered my life to Christ and became a Women of God. The God in me reflects the women in me who represents love. I am striving to be the women I have always desired to be in Christ. When I look at my life, I see my health, strength, faith, and a changed life. This is my beauty.

Life comes with no guarantees, no time outs and no promises. God has given me a chance to live my life over again, and this time it will not be wasted. There were plenty of times I felt like giving up, but I remembered that I have the power to move forward and not allow anyone or anything, bring me down. I was given another chance to live my life to the fullest and become a stronger vessel for my family.

I have come to realize that my husband and children need me to live and because of all I have been through, it is a sure thing that I am living proof that God can answer prayers and change lives for His Glory. I am a child of the Most High and He calls me to live and not die. Psalm 16:7-8 says, "I will bless The Lord who guides me; even at night my heart instructs me. I know The Lord is always with me. I will not be shaken, for he is right beside me."

My husband and my wonderful children have truly been a blessing in my life. When I was lost in my selfishness, they were there for me through thick and thin. We continue to build strong bonds through God together. James 5:16 says, "Therefore, confess your sins one to another, and pray for one another, so that you may be healed. The effective prayer of a righteous man can accomplish much."

Life is purely an adventure and the sooner we realize that, the sooner we will be able to treat life as a beautiful work of art. It's not selfish to love yourself nor is it selfish to take care of yourself by making your happiness a priority. This is my necessary struggle and I can only take it one day at a time. Right now as I am writing this I am 412 days clean. By the time you read this I will be beyond 600 days, and I thank God for every minute of them.

Have you ever awakened and felt tired and depressed about the direction your life was taking? You really desire things to change but you don't know where to begin. Are you afraid of what change might look like in your life? If you feel as though the world has never showed you any love; chances are there are many others who feel the same way. I have felt this way before.

One day in the mist of being drunk and strung out on drugs, I received a visit from an Angel who appeared to me in the form of my late grandmother in which I never had the opportunity to meet. I will never forget the words she spoke to me. "Be strong young women, you are better than that drug that had you." When I rose, I analyzed what had taken place; and it was in that very moment that I wanted to find myself. I needed to love myself even if others didn't.

I don't claim to have mastered life, but what I can say is that I have been delivered from my pain and from the struggle of recovering from drugs. I have even recovered from being sexually abused by a family member, and yet still I rise.

~Mavis J. Foster-Stephens

How do you define love? These days everyone has their own definition of what love means to them. Some people would see love as being an intense feeling of deep affection, but there is more to love than just intense affection. The defined word does not state anything about loving yourself. The world's view on love amongst others is warped.

Mark 12:31 says, we should love our neighbors as we would ourselves so if you love your-self, it should not be difficult to love others. If you love yourself, you would not cause harm to yourself nor would you neglect yourself. You would not starve yourself nor would you walk around smelly all day would you? This scripture is saying the same thing, if you will not cause harm to yourself, don't do it to others.

Everyone has a great need to be loved by someone. How would you feel if you were abandoned by your mother or your father? You would probably feel like your parents didn't want you right? The sad truth is that there are so many people dealing with these same issues on a daily basis. There are people in the world who think that they are only loved when people do things for them. This is a horrible way to live and think. A mindset change needs to take place. Love is not about people doing things for you.

David's Story

I was abandoned by my father when my mother passed away from Cancer. Many have walked this same path in life but I chose to share my story so that others would learn to love unconditionally like I have. I had to learn at an early age how to love myself because my dad was not around to show me. My father loves the idea of being a single man instead of staying home with me to be a real parent. My father left me in the hospital at my mother's bedside. This was the worst day of my life. I became a foster child right away to an elderly couple who lived a simple life. Whatever I needed, they were there for me and I appreciated them for that.

The elderly couple didn't talk much so I had to encourage myself many times. I tried to make friends at my new school but it I was looked at as being different because I was being raised by elderly people. I sat off in a corner by myself most days reading books about the rich and famous while the other children laughed and played. When I came home from school I would look in the mirror and say "I am somebody, I love you, and I am the greatest." I would do this every day. I also started feeling better about myself. I started to feel like I could conquer the world. I made sure all my work in school was done and I passed all of my classes. I graduated with honors because I made the honor roll every grading period.

Two weeks after I turned 17, the elderly couple I lived with, were killed in a car accident. I was away at college when I received the call. I went home to bury them and found out that there was a Will left behind for me. They never had any children so I was considered their only child. I was the new owner of the house and cars they owned. They also left me 8 million dollars. Wow, where did they get all that money from? I never even knew they had money like that. I was truly blessed beyond measure. All I ever wanted were parents to care for me.

The point of my story is as I got older I invested the money I received. I rented out my home and I purchased a nice 2 bedroom Condo. I felt great about where I was headed on life and I never stopped loving myself. I told myself every day that I loved me. I didn't want to think about my father leaving me because I wanted to love him anyway despite what he did. I thank God that he delivered me form abandonment issues. Men you must love yourselves to the fullest no matter what. Don't hold on to the past hurt and pain that others have caused you because it will follow you and you will not be able to have and attain healthy relationships with anyone.

The only scripture I have really focused on in the Bible is1Corinthians 1-13 where it speaks about love. Without love you have nothing. Let that marinate in your spirit. I pray that love takes over the heart of people all over the world and that my dad where ever he is, has found Christ and love because it's a beautiful thing.

Loving myself early on has helped me to be humble and not miserable and bitter. I believe it was the Holy Spirit that kept me in those trying times of my life. I didn't have time to focus on losing my mom and being abandoned by my dad because I had to love myself first. God wanted me to help others and not focus on the things that would keep me from my destiny. Many men are walking around with pride issues and pride destroys lives. When you love yourself to the fullest, you can love others with compassion and humility.

David is no different from anyone of us walking this earth. He did not allow his issues to keep him in bondage. He decided not to be bitter and angry but instead, love and forgive. It is amazing when you hear stories like David's. All too often men never tell their stories. Some are too prideful and think that loving themselves only pertains to woman and that is far from being the truth. Men have feelings too.

When you love yourself to the fullest, you are basically stripping yourself of everything negative and embracing yourself for who you are flaws and all. The negative aspect could be how people perceive you even if they don't know you. Often times we put more on ourselves than we could handle and it weighs us down just like negative energy. Your self-esteem should be high. For several of us, we let the everyday issues of life cause us to feel worthless and ugly inside out. Start telling yourself you are beautiful and do something nice for (you) every day even if it's one thing.

Thomas' Story

After being bullied, I started bullying others. I got in trouble every day at school because out it. I was teased and pushed around in the 6th grade. I was told I was too feminine to be around the boys at school. I was sexually assaulted and molested in the 5th grade by my uncle. He would hit me all the time and when I would scream out, he would tell me to stop screaming and shut up but the pain was too hard to bear. When my mother picked me up from his house after work, he would tell her that I was in a fight at school. Like so many other sexual abusers, he would threaten me if I told.

I started acting out in school because this would happen to me on a regular basis. I stayed in my room away from my mother a lot so that I didn't accidently tell her. I didn't want to take any chances with getting us killed. At School I would be called gay, homo and a fag. When I got mad I would punch a kid in the mouth just so the story could be legit about me actually getting into a fight. I started feeling bad inside. I looked in the mirror and thought nobody loved me. If they did, these bad things would not happen to me. When my mom saw me she would always say she loved me but I didn't believe her. She was so consumed with work that she never even noticed my sarcasm.

I was at the end of my 6th grade year when I met Mr. Lopez. He was my new guidance counselor for the new school year and he wanted to get acquainted with his students. He quickly noticed something different about me. I didn't want to be bothered. The last male figure I trusted, hurt me and I didn't want to subject myself to that again.

Mr. Lopez scheduled a meeting with me and asked me a few basic questions. After he was done, I was dismissed and scheduled for another meeting the next day. When I showed up he handed me a mirror and had me recite some things like my name and age. I also had to say I was strong and I have the victory over the enemy. What? I was told not to ask questions just repeat what he said. I had to say I love you to myself 20 times. Mr. Lopez did this for the remainder of the school year. I was getting frustrated because I was not allowed to ask questions.

Finally on the 90th day Mr. Lopez called me into his office and asked, "Do you have any questions for me?" My reply was "Well, I did weeks ago but I don't right now." I noticed that the last three months of school, my mother dropped me off and picked me up. Her shift was changed at work. She spent more time talking to me and helping me with my homework and cooking more for me. She really changed the way she did things and seemed to have a real interest in my life again. My uncle was arrested and I was relieved.

When I saw Mr. Lopez again, he asked me how I felt about myself. I actually felt great. I just needed to work on forgiving my uncle for violating me. My uncle never loved himself so he could not love me. Instead he violated me and caused harm to me. I am glad that it stopped when it did because I would have started to hate my mother for something she had no knowledge of.

I went to camp for the summer where my mom was my camp counselor. This camp had therapy sessions for youth and teens that had been hurt and abused in many ways. I learned a lot about loving myself fully and loving others the way God intended for us to love.

I thank Mr. Lopez for having showing an interest in me and helping me to see myself how God sees me who. I love myself no matter what has happened to me or what I have been through in my life. If Mr. Lopez had never seen the potential in me to love myself again, I am not sure where I would be today. I knew my mother loved me, it was hard to see that when she was always into her work. Since then my mother started taking me to church and I learned so much about love and Gods love for His people.

When I went to high school, I started a group for males called The Lovers of Christ. We went out and ministered love to other males who struggled with self-love and loving others. I kept it going in college also and we now have 150 members. As men, we need to

embrace ourselves with love. Love is the most important thing and the greatest to have.
My three favorite books in the Bible are Songs of Solomon, Proverbs and 1Corinthians 13. Check them out. I am sure my wife is happy that I did. Thanks to God for sending Mr. Lopez to help me walk in the light of love.

The one thing Thomas touched on was that his uncle did not love himself and he was right. How could he possibly give Thomas something that he didn't have? He couldn't. "You cannot give away something you don't have in you. We all need to accept ourselves, embrace our personalities, and our imperfections (Joyce Meyer)." If God did not want us to love ourselves, He wouldn't have created us out of love. In fact, God gave us His only begotten son who is Jesus, and He loved us so much that He died on the cross for us.

I encourage you to love yourself to the fullest in all that you do, from the time you wake up in the morning, until you prepare yourself for bed. You will feel refreshed and you will sleep well knowing that all day love was sent out into the atmosphere.
When you love yourself, you respect yourself and you don't worry about what others say because you are confident. Chances are most

people spread lies and rumors anyway but don't let that affect your mood to love yourself and other people unconditionally. If you learn to forgive and continue love, you are less likely to harbor un-forgiveness in your heart.

Two
You Are Beautiful

You are beautiful no matter what. This is something that men should also understand about themselves. Everyone should embrace themselves for who they are and how they look. What is your definition of true beauty? If you believe that in the beginning God created the heaven and the earth, how come you don't believe that He created you as well? God said what he created is good and beautiful so guess what? You are beautiful too.

This century is full of brainwashed people believing that they should have several types of surgeries to make them beautiful outwardly. Those things do not make one beautiful on the inside. The only way to change internally is by having the right mindset. Believe in yourself, believe that you are beautiful. How do you define what true beauty is?

Social media wants us to see ourselves looking skinny with packed on make-up to mask who we really are. Be who you were born to be not who the world wants you to be. When we allow others to dictate how we should look or feel we are setting ourselves up for heartache and failure. Let's just keep it real for a second here. This book is about the true beauty in you. The point in this is for you to love yourself and when others don't love you. You can still love yourself without being confined to the way the world wants to see you.

Who are you? What makes you who you are? How do you define yourself? Some people may have to really sit back and think about these questions but the truth is; when you know who you are, you don't have to think about it. You are Beautiful. I want you to say it over and over again and start really believing it because it's the truth. Repetition is the mother of success but not only that; you must believe what you say.

Do you wake up in the morning feeling bad sometimes? Why? Are you concerned about how people perceive you on the outside instead of what's in your heart? Let it go right now if this is how you feel. You have to love yourself, and you have to start motivating yourself.

The Bible says in Corinthians that if we don't have love, we don't have anything. As a flower blooms so do you. You are constantly changing into a better person. When you love yourself, it's easy to love others. There are many celebrities with great bodies who put on an act to make us believe they are happy, and many are not. Why are we obsessed with beauty to the point that we change the way we look, how we think, how we love, and who we should love?

Are you looking to be validated with superficial love? Why do we compromise ourselves in the name of love? Who told you that you were ugly? The answer is society. God created all humans and he created us to be beautiful. A woman is beautiful in every way imaginable. Song of Solomon is a beautiful love story but not only that, Solomon speaks about the beauty of a woman in which he takes as his bride.

Song of Solomon 4:1, 3, 4, 7

[1]How beautiful you are my darling! Oh, how beautiful!
[3]Your lips are like a secret ribbon; your mouth is lovely.
[4]Your neck is like the tower of David, built with elegance.
[7]All beautiful you are, my darling; there is no flaw in you.

Women are beautiful. You are beautiful. Think it, feel it, know it and embrace it. Solomon knew what he wanted and he saw the beauty in his bride. Women are supposed to be beautiful because this is how we were created. Love the skin you are in and if you feel you need to make changes with your weight, start exercising and eating right. If you want a new hairdo, get it done. Make yourself feel beautiful as well.

A woman's looks is not the only thing that should be considered to be beautiful. She should have a great attitude and confidence; she should also be intelligent and smart. Sometimes we may see a flower pot when we look in the mirror, and a man may see an expensive Vas that is so beautiful, that needs to be handled with care. There's more to inner and outer beauty.

Proverbs 11:16 states, "A kindhearted woman gains respect, but ruthless men only gain wealth." So what does this mean to you? The motives are not right for the man who wants to be wealthy. It never is. When you look at the word ruthless, it is understood as pathetic. A ruthless person has no compassion or pity for others. This is not an attribute that would make one beautiful. In fact, there is no beauty in ruthlessness. However, kindhearted people are sympathetic. This should be a characteristic of a beautiful person on the inside.

Proverbs 11: 22 states, "Like a gold ring in a pigs snout is a beautiful woman who shows no discretion." Interesting right? You can be a beautiful woman on the outside, but if you do not use discretion, your looks mean nothing. People will only see a gorgeous woman who doesn't value herself. We see it around us on a daily basis.

Do you have good judgment? How do we as woman value ourselves? Men, this question is for you as well. The answer is simple, dress with modesty, walk with integrity, speak with humility and use discernment in your daily life.

Get fit, stay in shape and dress to impress even if it's for you. Seeing women walk out of the house looking a hot mess is so unattractive. Your hair is all over your head; or you claim to have gone all natural but refuse to comb your hair. That is not considered an afro, it's a mess. You have to look like you're beautiful so that you can feel beautiful as well. A woman should always look like a woman. If you are a woman who looks, dresses and acts like a man, you should really re-evaluate what's going on in your life.

Where is your respect, your honor, your attractiveness? The world should be able to see these things when they look at you. You should strive to be a woman who is so beautiful and full of confidence. It's time to start loving yourself enough to look and feel beautiful.

People look up to you and you have many roles. If you are walking around stressed and depressed because June Bug called you ugly, you will never be able to accomplish your true goals because you are always concerned and focused on what someone is saying about you.

Do you want to better yourself? There are many ways you can do that as beautiful as you are. Proverbs 31; speaks about how a woman is able to do many things. God has equipped us for this so we should be doing it. Ask yourself are you growing in every area of your life? If not, it's really time to make some changes. You are capable to do many things. God has blessed you with many talents. He has spelled some out for you in Proverbs 31:10-31.

Epilogue: The Wife of Noble Character

¹⁰A wife of noble character who can find?
  She is worth far more than rubies.
¹¹ Her husband has full confidence in her
  and lacks nothing of value.
¹² She brings him good, not harm,
  all the days of her life.
¹³ She selects wool and flax
  and works with eager hands.
¹⁴ She is like the merchant ships,
  bringing her food from afar.
¹⁵ She gets up while it is still night;
  she provides food for her family
  and portions for her female servants.
¹⁶ She considers a field and buys it;
  out of her earnings she plants a vineyard.
¹⁷ She sets about her work vigorously;
  her arms are strong for her tasks.
¹⁸ She sees that her trading is profitable,
  and her lamp does not go out at night.
¹⁹ In her hand she holds the distaff
  and grasps the spindle with her fingers.
²⁰ She opens her arms to the poor
  and extends her hands to the needy.
²¹ When it snows, she has no fear for her
household;
  for all of them are clothed in scarlet.
²² She makes coverings for her bed;
  she is clothed in fine linen and purple.
²³ Her husband is respected at the city gate,
  where he takes his seat among the elders of

the land.

²⁴ She makes linen garments and sells them,
and supplies the merchants with sashes.

²⁵ She is clothed with strength and dignity;
she can laugh at the days to come.

²⁶ She speaks with wisdom,
and faithful instruction is on her tongue.

²⁷ She watches over the affairs of her household
and does not eat the bread of idleness.

²⁸ Her children arise and call her blessed;
her husband also, and he praises her.

²⁹ "Many women do noble things,
but you surpass them all."

³⁰ Charm is deceptive, and beauty is fleeting;
but a woman who fears the LORD is to be praised.

³¹ Honor her for all that her hands have done,
and let her works bring her praise at the city gate.

This is not just for married woman. This is for all the women in the world. Growth is always important and this also makes a woman beautiful. When you are constantly growing in every area of your life and developing the gifts and talents that God gave you; this make you more beautiful. It's not always about outer beauty.

More than a Woman

You are more than just a woman. You are a beautiful being. God designed you specifically for His purpose and for man to be amazed by. You have so many amazing qualities and God sees your beauty differently from anyone in the world. You are important to God. 1Peter 3:3-4 states, [3] "Your beauty should not come from outward adornment, such as elaborate hairstyles and the wearing of gold jewelry or fine clothes. [4] Rather, it should be that of your inner self, the unfading beauty of a gentle and quiet spirit, which is of great worth in God's sight."

This type of beauty is very valuable. Some woman hide behind the make-up and the hair especially when the have awful attitudes. Your beauty will shine and stand out no matter what you are wearing and your inner beauty enhances your outer beauty. You should be a woman that is slow to anger and patient. You should be a woman who doesn't like to argue and keep up confusion. You should be a woman that has peace. This is beautiful to God. Do you know what else God loves about the beautiful woman He designed? He loves the fact that a beautiful woman does not see herself as equal to men, nor does she compete with them. She is submissive, understanding, gentle, valuable, and she knows her strengths.

Submission

Some of you are probably thinking about the word submissive. Some of you may have even gotten an attitude just hearing that word but drop all those bad things that you heard, read, or even saw that pertain to submission and let's look at it from a different view point.

The dictionary states that submission is the action or fact of accepting or yielding to a superior force or to the will or authority of another person. Superior is defined as high in rank, status or quality and higher in position. When a woman is married God wants us to submit ourselves to our husbands. When we do this, we are not to shut up, we are not to be controlled, and we are not to be abused.

When God tells us to submit to Him, sometimes we question certain aspects of it. Do you believe God is controlling us by telling us what we should be doing? If you can submit to God, you can submit to your husband because your husband is supposed to follow the will of God. When your husband is following Gods will, so are you. A man who submits to God will talk to their wife about things to see what her views are on the subject matter. When you yield to your husband, you understand what has been established by God. Keep in mind that submitting to God also mean being obedient in the workplace, home and school, etc.

Ephesians 5:22-32

[22] <u>Wives, submit yourselves to your own husbands as you do to the Lord.</u> [23] For the husband is the head of the wife as Christ is the head of the church, his body, of which he is the Savior. [24] Now as the church submits to Christ, so also wives should submit to their husbands in everything. [25] <u>Husbands, love your wives, just as Christ loved the church and gave himself up for her</u> [26] to make her holy, cleansing her by the washing with water through the word, [27] and to present her to himself as a radiant church, without stain or wrinkle or any other blemish, but holy and blameless. [28] <u>In this same way, husbands ought to love their wives as their own bodies. He who loves his wife loves himself.</u> [29] After all, no one ever hated their own body, but they feed and care for their body, just as Christ does the church, [30] for we are members of his body. [31] "For this reason a man will leave his father

and mother and be united to his wife and the two will become one flesh."

As you can see, submission is not what you may have thought it to be. In these passages, it also points out love, self-love and loving others. All of this is designed to be beautiful in the eyes of God because He ordained this. The bottom line is God honors a woman who puts Him first in her life and one who is humble, patient and knows how to serve. This doesn't make you beneath a man. You are beautiful because of the characteristics, gifts and talents God gave you and when you submit to Him, you will have no problem submitting to the man of God that is placed in your life.

From now on when you think about your beauty think about all the things a woman can do such as carrying and delivering a child, nursing, and multitasking. You can do all these things and this is a beauty that is so powerful and valuable to God. This is a part of the True Beauty in you.

Three
How to Look and Feel the Part

Have you ever experienced a sleepless night? If so did you wake up cranky? Did the rest of your day determine how your night went? Many of us have experienced this and have taken the irritation of a sleepless night to work with us. The first thing is to get enough rest at night so that you can wake up feeling refreshed and ready to start your day. When you get up tell God thank you for life and say out loud, "Today and every day is the best day of my life because Jesus lives big in me." Embrace that and feel it. Tell yourself you are beautiful.

Steps

1. Good hygiene before leaving the house.

2. Comb your hair and make it look nice and presentable because you never know who you will run into that can help you get to the next level in your life.

3. Wear make-up ladies. If you can't make sure you use daily moisturizer and add a tint of color to your lips. You will still

look nice and presentable. Natural is always good.

4. Have a positive attitude when you leave the house. People can feel your vibes whether it's good or bad.

5. Command the atmosphere. Call out the things you want and what you expect God to do. Feel good about it. Remember what you put out into the atmosphere is what you will receive back.

6. Speak with authority.

7. Walk with confidence.

8. Love unconditionally.

These steps will help you to feel good about yourself and you will also look good as well. There's nothing like feeling beautiful on the inside out and living it every day.

Hygiene

Some people may think this is crazy but the Bible speaks about cleansing from many aspects. Much of it has to do with the spiritual aspect. God wants us to be clean inside and outside whether we want to believe it or not. How do you walk around as a beautiful woman smelling like a pile of old nasty rotten garbage? It is an unpleasant. Even Jesus washed the disciple's feet at the last supper. This has to do with servant-hood but I needed you to get the point. Wash your clothes so that you can look the part of being and smelling clean as well as presentable.

The Look

Looking presentable means so many things to so many people. Some people think that it is alright to walk out of the house looking a mess. Wearing wrinkled clothing, dressing sloppy, and not combing their hair is not presentable and people will treat you the way you look.

Attitude

Your attitude means everything whether you think so or not. When you leave your home, you should have a positive attitude. No one wants to run into someone who is angry all the time and doesn't know how to talk to people. People are watching how you respond, look and act. Make the best of every moment because little Suzy may want to be like you when she grows up. Start your day off with positive affirmations and believe in them.

The Atmosphere

Here it is again, command the atmosphere. Call the things you want and what you expect God to do into existence. Feel good about it and have confidence. Remember what you put out in the atmosphere is what you will receive back, good or bad. Take that positive energy and work it.

Speaking with Authority

You have to be willing to say what you mean and mean what you say. Speak with authority and make sure that power goes forth to enforce what it is you need and want. This can also be about demanding respect. Do not let people run all over you.

Walking with Confidence

It's time to stop holding your head down when you speak or even walk. Believe that you can do whatever you set your mind to and go for it. You should always be confident about your abilities and who you are as well as the qualities you possess.

Loving Unconditionally

Unconditional love is defined in the dictionary as affection without any limitations. It is also love without conditions. Do you love without people conditions? If you don't, maybe it is time to change your mindset. Make loving yourself first and unconditionally apart of your mindset change.

It is time for a new you, a new look and you must look and feel beautiful. Look prosperous even if you think you are not at the time. The more you look the part, the more it will become a reality. You will soon find yourself being prosperous in many ways.

Love Yourself

Surround yourself with beauty, and people that are like-minded. If you like to decorate, do it. Adding some flowers or pictures and some great aroma will spark happiness inside of you. When you love yourself, you have self-confidence. People love hanging around others who have confidence.

Be Grateful

Be thankful and grateful for what God has done for you and all that you have. You are blessed and when you are grateful and thankful, many doors of opportunity starts opening up for you.

Stay Positive

I cannot express this enough. Start getting excited about the new adventures you will be a part of. Embrace your beauty, embrace life and love. Embrace others even if they are different from you. Be willing to learn and try new things.

Be Happy

It's time that you keep a smile on your face even through tough times. Appreciate all of your flaws and work on them to become a better you.

Posture

Stop slouching. Keep your shoulder back and your head up and walk like you are on the Cover Girl Runway ladies. Make sure when you stand, you are standing straight. You do not want lower back issues because of bad posture. Also good posture makes your clothes look good on you and you appear to be smaller in certain clothing.

Exercise and Eat Right

Take vitamins, drink plenty of water and eat the right foods. When you exercise you feel better and you will also begin to look better as well.

Get plenty of rest

When you get the proper rest, it reduces your stress levels, you don't have anxiety and your body is not tense all the time. When you do not get enough rest, you start to look older than your age and you become sluggish all the time. You can see and feel the difference by the way your skin looks and feels.

Good Hygiene

Stay clean all the time and smelling good. This will also help you feel beautiful. Keep your hair done, take care of your skin and nails and make sure you brush your teeth and keep good smelling breath.

Flawless Make-up Ladies

If you wear make-up, it is important to wear your make-up naturally in the day time and a little dramatic in the evening because of lighting. Keep in mind that dramatic doesn't necessarily mean wearing your make-up like it's a mask. You still want it to look nice and beautiful. Don't over-do it.

Taking care of your skin means making sure you are not using dirty brushes, old lip stick, powders, foundation and mascara. This can cause infection, clogged pores and pimples.

Get rid of bad habits

Anything that can make you feel down that is not positive especially health wise, you should stop doing it. If you smoke and you find yourself out of breath often and it is keeping you from exercising, maybe it's time to put that down. It makes your skin look dry and ages you. You Love yourself right? So it's time to let that go.

Love Others

When you love others, the characteristics of God are flowing through you. The gift of love from God is such a wonderful thing and we need to give it to others. Do you feel good when you do something good for others? Sometimes all people need is a hug or a smile, and maybe a word of encouragement to let them know that it will be alright. Start walking in love from now on.

Love yourself from God's point of view which means you should see yourself as God sees you. Value yourself as God values you and when you start doing this, loving others unconditionally will come naturally like loving yourself. When you have an awesome love for yourself, you tend to love others, inspire, empower, encourage and acknowledge those who need it as well as those who have lifted you up in your time of need. This shows great love and appreciation.

Compliment your body

You are beautiful and so is the body that God gave you. You may have had children or even a medical issue that has caused you to gain weight. You can still look gorgeous in those fabulous clothes. Whatever size you are, rock what you wear and wear it with style. Always wear clothing that compliments your body type and your skin tone because this will make you look good in what you wear. Dress in clothing that will not make you look like an old maid. You do not want to walk around looking like you need a makeover every other week so dress to impress all the time.

Judging and Favoritism

Whether you believe it or not, people judge you by your appearance. People treat you how you look and the worst part about it is; they are so blatant with how they do it these days. It's not as complicated as it seems. Some women don't mind leaving the house looking unprofessional, but others do. When you want more for yourself, you can demand more from others.

There are many people who have been mistreated or over looked because of their outer appearance. The Bible speaks on this issue in which many of us have experienced this at least one time in our lives including myself.

James 2:1-4

My brothers and sisters, believers in our glorious Lord Jesus Christ must not show favoritism. [2] Suppose a man comes into your meeting wearing a gold ring and fine clothes, and a poor man in filthy old clothes also comes in. [3] If you show special attention to the man wearing fine clothes and say, "Here's a good seat for you," but say to the poor man, "You stand there" or "Sit on the floor by my feet," [4] have you not discriminated among yourselves and become judges with evil thoughts?

It was a Sunday afternoon and I was dressed in a black t-shirt and grey sweat pants. I had to go to the laundry mat so I decided to get the detergent from the store next to the laundry mat. My hair was not all over my head it was combed down and it was neat. There were two cashiers but one decided that he would talk and not take customers. There were two people ahead of me. The cashier saw me and looked me in my eyes and kept talking to the other cashier. I thought to myself, why was he just standing there running off at the mouth instead of opening the register to check customers out. To my surprise, there was a young lady walking up behind me all dressed up with flawless hair and make-up. She looked as though she had just left church or was going on a date.

As she walked up to get behind me, the cashier said in a low voice, "I can take you right here." She proudly walked up to his register and checked out. I thought to myself "Wow, are you kidding me?" A few seconds after the young lady walked out, someone walked up to the register and the cashier said "I'm not open, but she can take you over there." I don't believe I looked like a bum that day but since I didn't look the "part", I was over looked. There was nothing special about the young lady who was serviced before me. She just looked the part.

Sounds silly huh? Well this is how life is. People tend to take you more serious based on your appearance and how you speak. It's called profiling to a degree. Everyone has been profiled at one time or another even if you didn't realize it.

The point is, how you present yourself to the world, is how you will be perceived and treated. Sometimes we can cause our own selves to miss out on a blessing. If you look good, you will feel good and chances are, you will also speak positive and send off positive energy to everyone around you.
Knowing how to speak is also beautiful. It would not be nice at all to be beautiful on the outside but when you open your mouth to speak, it's a different story. Many women have the beauty part down but the intelligence and

smarts is missing. This is a quick way to become very unattractive in many ways.

There are many cases where there are no evil thoughts behind the favoritism but in most cases there are. You get the point though right? In chapter 2 of James, he condones the act of favoritism. Most people as you have seen treat well-dressed people better than someone who would appear to look shabby. Some people do this because they want to identify with successful people.

The point is, present yourself in a manner in which you would like to be treated and because you are beautiful, always look that way. If you don't feel the part and you leave your home and someone treats you unfairly, it will make you feel worse than you look. Beauty is inside out wear it well.

Four
Self-Esteem and Confidence
(True Beauty)

Genesis 1:27 states, "So God created man in his own image; in the image of God He created him; male and female He created them."

The defined word of self-esteem from the dictionaries standpoint is this; self-esteem is a term used in sociology and psychology to reflect a person's overall emotional evaluation of his or her own worth. It is a judgment of oneself as well as an attitude towards (the self).

How do you feel about yourself? Feeling good about yourself means removing "you" from having a low self-esteem. When you were a baby, you came into the world with personality and characteristic traits that only belong to you. You were able to explore life as you grew older and began to develop an understanding about self-worth, morals and values. You will begin to learn more about yourself and make decisions based on your likes and dislikes. You began to see the world with a set of new eyes as you experience what life has to offer you.

During these critical times in our lives we start to grow and become more aware of our self-esteem and either how to improve it or how to make it stronger. Unfortunately, many fall by the side of the road lost, hurt and confused about what they should do next or which way they should be going. People have a way of stripping you of your confidence or worth. It is a daily journey building and keeping your self-esteem intact. These steps will help you build your confidence and boost your self-esteem.

It Starts on the Inside

Many people will come into your life trying to convince you that you are not beautiful and you are nothing. The Devil is a liar. He wants you to believe these things. If you buy into them, he has you right where he wants you and his intentions are to kick you hard to bring you down. What you believe about yourself is important. Do not allow others to convince you that you are worthless.

Affirmations

In an earlier chapter I stated that you should look in the mirror and tell yourself you are beautiful and say I love you; you can also say things like this:

- I am the head and not the tail: (Deuteronomy 28:13), "The Lord will make you the head, not the tail. If you pay attention to the commands of the Lord your God that I give you this day and carefully follow them, you will always be at the top, never at the bottom."

- I am fearfully and wonderfully made: (Psalm 139:14), "I praise you because I am fearfully and wonderfully made; your works are wonderful, I know that full well."

- I am prosperous: (Deuteronomy 28:11), "The Lord will grant you abundant prosperity in the fruit of your womb, the young of your livestock and the crops of your ground in the land he swore to your ancestors to give you."

- I can have what I say I can have: (Mark 11:24), "Therefore I tell you, whatever you ask for in prayer, believe that you have received it, and it will be yours."

- I am happy: (Ecclesiastes 3:12), "I know that there is nothing better for men than to be happy and do good while they live."

- I can do anything I put my mind to do: (Philippians 4:13), "I can do everything through Christ who gives me strength." You get the point right? Make up some affirmations and say them but believe them as well. This will boost your confidence and self-esteem. Learn how to forgive yourself as well as others.

Build your Confidence

Confidence is defined as a feeling of self-assurance arising from one's appreciation of one's own abilities or qualities. Be confident in who you are, in your abilities. When you start off small, you will soon build an empire before you know it. Baby steps never hurt anyone. In fact, sometimes in life we have to start over so that we can be where we desire to be and in starting over, there are things we must let go of.

Start making smarter choices about who you spend your valuable time with and the things you are hearing and saying. Little things can cause big improvements.

Self Improvement

You have to start trusting yourself in every area of your life. Please your self meaning; stop trying to please everyone else in your life because that's what they want you to do. What do you want? Other people can be considered at times but not to the point where you lose yourself to what everyone else wants from you. People pleasing can weigh you down leaving you unhappy.

Sometimes we find ourselves bending over backward for people and when we need help, they are nowhere to be found or they just will not help you. You will worry yourself sick being stressed out because people will not return the favor.

Be yourself. Do not try to imitate others because you will never get it right. You are special and you have your own gifts and talents. You should never want to be like anyone else or live the life someone else is living. You never know what a person is going through. The grass is not always greener on the other side. 2 Corinthians 10:12 states, "We do not dare to classify or compare ourselves with some who commend themselves. When they measure themselves by themselves and compare themselves with themselves, they are not wise." You do not want to be in this vain. This has to do with conceit and no love for others.

While improving and loving yourself, constantly think positive thoughts. Develop the "I can do all things" mindset; live it and love it. Learn how to appreciate yourself to the fullest. Know your strengths and your weaknesses and work on improving and building the other. Practice makes perfect so develop good habits and incorporate them into your daily life. Stop allowing people to define who you are and focus on your qualities.

Be creative and do some things that you have never done before. Take a trip to your favorite place, read a book that you've always wanted to read. Stay busy by doing positive things. Go help out in a shelter or at church. Build other people up and encourage them. A smile goes a long way. Believe in yourself.

Adam's Story

I share my story because I had a bad habit of treating women like they were beneath me. I had three ladies in which I called my women at once. All were under the impression that they were the only ones. I did not respect any of them. I didn't even like them enough to respect them. I felt bad about it six months after it all ended because of what my sister went through.

My goal was to have many women and get them to do anything I asked them to do. I preyed on the ones who looked like they didn't have any self-esteem. I never hit a woman but I have called them a few names here and there. I didn't care about their feelings because I didn't have any myself. I didn't love my self so I was unable to love and show love to anyone else. The day came when my sister had a boyfriend who hit her and pushed her around. He got her pregnant and he slept around on her. Similar to what I was doing.

I had an awesome childhood. My mom and dad have a good relationship and to my knowledge, my dad has never cursed my mother or hit her. I started hanging out with the wrong people and needed some excitement in my life and unfortunately, it was the wrong kind. My self-esteem dropped and I did everything under the sun just to get attention.

I realized that this was not who I really was. I had to talk some sense into my sister and I had to change my life. I had to eventually go to each woman I hurt and tell her I was sorry and hope that would forgive me enough to start over building a friendship instead of being lovers. I literally had to examine myself and probe my ways and return to the Lord (Lamentations 3:40).

I was a fool to allow myself to treat those women in such a way. I acted like I hated myself. I started dressing like I didn't care and talking like I was uneducated. If my sister had not gone through what she did, I may have continued this journey of hate for a long time. I am glad the Lord woke me up and allowed me to experience what I was doing first hand.

Men need to love themselves as well. If we continue to walk around mistreating women and abusing them, we are making a bold statement saying that women mean nothing to us and that we don't love ourselves. We must love ourselves and take pride in ourselves without being prideful.

It was clear that when I realized the lack of confidence these women had, it was easy for me to treat them however I wanted to. Everything has a cause and effect. I didn't think about any of the females in my family when I decided to go on that hateful rampage. When it hits home, people start to rethink their actions. I am truly sorry for what I did and I made a vow not to allow myself to succumb to other people's foolishness even if it's for laughs.

Women are beautiful. Humans are beautiful. We are a masterpiece made by an awesome God and no one can duplicate His wonderful art. Love yourselves, and love others the way God intended for us to be loved. Love is an action word!

Adam realizes that what God created is beautiful. Sometimes men find themselves in prideful situations. Men have feelings just like females do but men have a different way of showing them. There is nothing wrong with being a confident man. In fact, a woman loves a confident man. There are many ways to be confident and carry your-self with great esteem. The key is in your possession but it is up to you to unlock the door to your own happiness. Beauty starts on the inside and you have to believe in your confidence and know that you are beautiful inwardly and outwardly.

Your self-esteem is great it defines you. Your confidence is beautiful just like you are so inspire others by the way you walk, look, positivity; and when you enter the room, heads will turn. Be confident and know what you want and do not allow others to dictate what you should have or what you should be doing with your life.

Five
No More Abuse
(Mentally, Emotionally, Verbally, & Physically)

Proverbs 6:16-19

[16] There are six things the LORD hates,
    seven that are detestable to him
[17] haughty eyes, a lying tongue,
     hands that shed innocent blood,
[18] a heart that devises wicked schemes, feet
that are quick to rush into evil,
[19] a false witness who pours out lies and a
person who stirs up conflict in the community.

The scripture Proverbs 6:16-19, spells out all sorts of abuse. These are things the Lord hates. If the Lord hates abuse, we should as well. Who wants to be in any type of relationship that displays such things? I don't and I'm sure you don't either. These things in relationships are detrimental. A person cannot function when surrounded by lies, schemes and physical abuse. How then do you consider your-self beautiful if you cannot see the beauty in you because of the blindfold of lies that you wear?

Mental, verbal, and emotional abuse makes one feel unloved, inadequate, undeserving and undesired. Add physical abuse to that and it's a wrap. Your whole world seems to be crumbling. Some people are abusive because of the environment they grew up in. It is hard to see a child suffer because of their home life was filled with abuse. Some parents even provoke their children. These things are generational curses that carry on from one generation to the next and if no one is praying that these curses be broken, they are re-lived and more people become hurt from it.

Ephesians 6:1-10

Children, obey your parents in the Lord, for this is right. [2] "Honor your father and mother," which is the first commandment with promise: [3] "that it may be well with you and you may live long on the earth." [4] And you, fathers, do not provoke your children to wrath, but bring them up in the training and admonition of the Lord. [5] Bondservants, be obedient to those who are your masters according to the flesh, with fear and trembling, in sincerity of heart, as to Christ; [6] not with eye-service, as men-pleasers, but as bondservants of Christ, doing the will of God from the heart, [7] with goodwill doing service, as to the Lord, and not to men, [8] knowing that whatever good anyone does, he will receive the same from the Lord, whether *he is* a slave or free. [9] And you, masters, do the same things to them, giving up threatening, knowing that your own Master also is in heaven, and there is no partiality with Him.[10] Finally, my brethren, be strong in the Lord and in the power of His might.

You are worth more than that. You can be strong. There is a popular phrase used all the time and I am sure you have heard of it. "People can only do to you, what you allow them to." This is true. If you do not stand up for yourself, people will take advantage. No more abuse starts now. We have talked about love and loving others but we have not touched on the abuse most people have endured to cause them to stop loving themselves and caring for others. There is a multitude of people suffering from all types of abuse from rape, molestation, domestic and so much more.

I want you to be free from the hurt and pain in your life, so you must give all of these burdens to the Lord. There is a way for you to be free again, and you can conquer anything.

Understanding that there are deep rooted seeds of hate in the lives of people will help us to pray accordingly and deal with people in love. Since you have been built up and inspired as well as encouraged, you can walk in love. It's time to see the beauty in you as well as in others.

Stop allowing people to mentally control your mind, emotions, thoughts and your heart. No more verbal abuse. You are smart and courageous and you do not have to endure any type of abuse from anyone. Abusive people are all over the world in every culture. Some of them even appear to be nice but that is deception and you must use discernment when dealing with anyone. Sometimes it is hard for a person to remove themselves from an abusive environment because of fear.

There are two definitions that define fear: [1]an unpleasant emotion caused by the belief that someone or something is dangerous, likely to cause pain, or a threat.

[2] Being afraid of someone or something as likely to be dangerous, painful, or threatening. Both definitions have similar meanings. You can control fear. When you allow your emotions to invade the atmosphere, people can

sense that. Some people will use it against you. Normally they can tell if you are a strong and confident person by the first incident.

Never show any signs weakness. When people don't know what's going on in your mind, it kind of scares them. Fighting will only make things worse and you do not want to stoop to their level. Deuteronomy 32:35 says, "It is mine to avenge; I will repay. In due time their foot will slip; their day of disaster is near and their doom rushes upon them."

Fear can creep up on you and paralyze you from leaving if you become weak. Fear can keep you in bondage. Those who instill fear in others have no love for themselves. How can they love you without self-love? John 13:34 says, "A new command I give you: Love one another as I have loved you, so you must love one another." This concept is not hard to grasp but because so many of us have been through so much, love seems to be so far-fetched.

Many people are abusive because they have been abused and have not experience real love. In fact, they have low self-esteem and lack self-love.
We must have the right mindset to change our situations. Love, positive self-esteem and

confidence is very important to display in your life. There are many people walking around settling for less. When you settle, you tend to get involved with people who do not have your best interest at heart. Selfish people only think of themselves and what they feel is important to them and when this happens, it is easy to abuse and use others with no regard of how someone else is feeling. The "About Me" syndrome is running rapid all over the world.

Abuse is surrounded by selfishness. Many people take advantage of others because they do not know how to deal with people. We must renew our minds and always remember that love conquers all.

"Do not conform to the pattern of this world, but be transformed by the renewing of your mind. Then you will be able to test and approve what God's will is; his good, pleasing and perfect will (Romans 12:2)."

Types of Abuse (according to the Dictionary) Defined

- **Mental abuse:** Psychological abuse, also referred to as emotional abuse or mental abuse, is a form of abuse characterized by a person subjecting or exposing another to behavior that may result in psychological trauma, including anxiety, chronic depression, or post-traumatic stress disorder.

- **Emotional abuse:** Any kind of abuse that is emotional rather than physical in nature. It can include anything from verbal abuse and constant criticism to more subtle tactics, such as intimidation, manipulation, and refusal to ever be pleased.

- **Verbal abuse:** The excessive use of language to undermine someone's dignity and security through insults or humiliation, in a sudden or repeated manner.

- **Physical abuse:** is an act of another party involving contact intended to cause feelings of physical pain, injury, or other physical suffering or bodily harm.

There are four types of abuse displayed in those who are abusers. Its time you take back your life and stand up for yourself. If you wait on the abuser to repair the damage they have caused, you will be waiting a long time. Don't get me wrong here, abusers can be delivered and change their lives; many have. Jesus can heal every wound you have including the wounds of the abuser.

2 Timothy 3:1-8 says, "But understand this, that in the last days there will come times of difficulty. For people will be lovers of self, lovers of money, proud, arrogant, abusive, disobedient to their parents, ungrateful, unholy, heartless, unappeasable, slanderous, without self-control, brutal, not loving good, treacherous, reckless, swollen with conceit, lovers of pleasure rather than lovers of God, having the appearance of godliness, but denying its power. Avoid such people."

Abusive controlling people are selfish. No matter what you do for them, it's never enough. They are never happy. Awareness will help you change your life so that you will not continue to be a victim. Today many people are experiencing 2 Timothy 3:1-8 even as we see it. The Lord wants us to be aware of these things and stay away from them. People have no respect for each other in this century like they use to. This is why it is important to love God, love your-self, and love others.

It's time to love your-self again, and forgive again. You must learn to forgive others as well as yourself. Don't be so hard on yourself and don't beat yourself up because you were in a situation that you never thought you'd be in. You are still beautiful and always will be. No more strongholds you are free. Walk in your healing and deliverance. Walk with your head held high. Smile again you deserve it.

Psalm 147:3 says, "He heals the brokenhearted and binds up their wounds." Yes the Lord can do that for you but you must believe that. Where your shirt proudly "No More Abuse!" and mean every word of it. Now that you have decided to be free, surround yourself with people that can help you. Take it one day at a time and start realizing that your body is not a playground nor is it a punching bag. Understanding that people who have been deeply hurt have a tendency to hurt and abuse others will put things in perspective on how you view people through God's eyes.

No more abuse means not entertaining negative conversations and company as well as corrupt language. You need positive influences around you. Ephesians 4:29-32 says, "Do not let any unwholesome talk come out of your mouths, but only what is helpful for building others up according to their needs, that it may benefit those who listen. And do not grieve the Holy Spirit of God, with whom you were sealed for the day of redemption. Get rid of all bitterness, rage and anger, brawling and slander, along with every form of malice. Be kind and compassionate to one another, forgiving each other, just as in Christ God forgave you."

Your heart has been through enough, even if you have not been physically abused. As you have seen, abuse takes many forms and if you have ever been on a journey where you have contemplated suicide, or felt ugly and un-loved for any reason, you have experienced a form of abuse in some shape or fashion. No more abuse has to do with you changing your mindset about you and your life. It is time for a new path and a new journey so that you can empower others all over the world. God sees the good in you. He also sees the beauty in you. You don't have to go purchase a new body to prove that you are beautiful. Love what you have and embrace it.

When people get surgeries to make themselves look more presentable to the world, what they are really saying is that "I don't love myself the way God created me." The bottom line is you have reached your breaking point and now you can start changing your life. Not only that, you can help others change their lives as well. You have had a season of being stagnant and now you are in a season of power, empowerment, motivation, courage and strength. Stand firm knowing in your heart that everything about you is confident and beautiful.

Love yourself to the fullest because you are beautiful. You are awesome and confident. Wear your breast plate of righteousness proudly. No More Abuse!

www.ingramcontent.com/pod-product-compliance
Lightning Source LLC
Chambersburg PA
CBHW060708030426
42337CB00017B/2797